**Genre** Nonfic...

 Essential Ques....
How do people work with animals?

by Justin Yong

CHAPTER 1

How Do You Teach a Dog?

Dogs love to play!

Dogs make great pets! They follow rules if people teach them. Would you like to be a dog teacher? It's hard work, but it's fun.

If a dog behaves well, give a small treat. Then say, "Good dog!"

Give lots of love. You will get love back!

This dog knows the rules.

This girl pats the dog after it sits.

"Sit! Stay! Come!"

These are key words a dog should know.

First, teach a dog to sit. Gently push the dog's back end down and say, "Sit!"

If it stands up, say "Sit!" If it sits, give it a treat.

Now teach the dog to stay. Have the dog sit. Put out your hand and say, "Stay!"

Next, walk a few steps away. If the dog stays, give her a treat.

Then say, "Come!" If she comes, give her a treat for being so clever.

This dog is learning to stay.

CHAPTER 2
How Can a Dog Teach You?

This dog is shy or scared.

This dog is begging.

A dog can't talk, of course. So he will give a signal instead.

If a dog's paw is out, he wants something. What if his tail is down? It's a sign that he's sad.

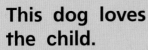

This dog loves the child.

This dog wants to play.

If a dog is wagging his tail, he's happy. If his rear end is up, he wants to play.

What if he rolls onto his back? He's saying, "You're the boss. Please rub my tummy!"

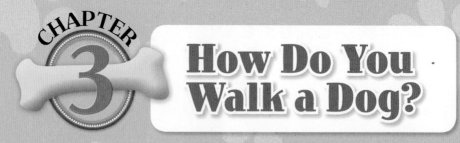

CHAPTER 3
How Do You Walk a Dog?

These dogs are learning to use a leash.

Dogs love to go for walks! First, clip on the leash.

Walk slowly. Try not to pull on the leash. But do keep the dog near you.

Sometimes a dog pulls on the leash. She might have found something to sniff!

Stop walking. When she is still, you can start walking again.

This dog is pulling.

This dog likes to run!

You can run with a dog too. But if she pants too much, slow down or stop. Make sure you and the dog take a water break!

If you'd like, you can write down all the rules. Then you can help someone else teach a dog!

You can write a list of ways to train your dog.

Respond to Reading

Retell

Use the chart to help you retell *Teach a Dog!*

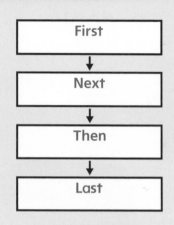

First
↓
Next
↓
Then
↓
Last

Text Evidence

1. Look at pages 4 and 5. What can you teach a dog after it learns to sit? Sequence

2. Look at page 8. What is the first thing to do before you walk a dog? Sequence

3. Is *Teach a Dog!* fiction or nonfiction? Why? Genre

Compare Texts
Read about how animals work with people.

Working with Dolphins

Dolphins can understand commands.

Did you know that dolphins are good helpers? They can help people with special needs. Dolphins can help people who are sick or hurt too.

The woman in the photo trains dolphins. She teaches them how to swim with children.

Dolphins like to eat fish.

Trainers teach dolphins how to do tricks. A dolphin can stand on its tail! Some dolphins can jump through hoops. Watching tricks makes people happy.

Make Connections

Look at both stories. How do people train animals? Text to Text

Focus on
Social Studies

Purpose To find out the most liked pet

What to Do

Step 1 Take a survey. Find out what kind of pets your classmates like.

Step 2 Tally the answers.

Step 3 Share the answers with the class.